God's Perfect Peace In Action

This is an incredible journey of 28 years, starting with a prayer in search of God. The writer then gives testimony to how God's peace has motivated and enriched his life.

The writer starts his story when he is 26 years of age. At that time he was a factory worker with a good salary, beautiful girlfriend of 3 years (who was his fiancée) and plenty of friends.

Then suddenly he felt a deep desire to pray and ask if God existed. Within a short time he starts to read a Sunday newspaper Christian column, where he is told about how much Jesus loves him. The writer wrestles with these completely new ideas, and then finds faith.

The message touches his heart like nothing has before. God tells him to leave his girlfriend. He is made redundant twice! Then feels God has something special for him to do.

Having left school with no qualifications he enrols at college, which he finances himself. In the first year he receives a special award for most improved student. In the second year he receives a City & Guilds Certificate in management.

After college comes Bible College, then back to college for "A" levels. Finally, he arrives at University and gains a B.A. in Theology with honours.

Throughout the story the writer continuously states that, it is God's peace that drives him to new areas in life. He continuously seeks fulfilment of Ephesians 2:10 "For we are

God's workmanship created in Christ Jesus to do good works which God prepared in advance for us to do."

He takes the reader on a journey as he searches for God's will in his life. He has many jobs. He moves home with his family to assist a minister in a Church of England. He in fact is interviewed for the ministry. He enrols on a P.G.C.E course to teach R.E., nothing however seems to settle his spirit.

Finally, he believes he finds the works that God has for him. This job, he has had for thirteen years. He never wants to retire, and believes it is essential for every Christian to find a fulfilment for Eph 2:10 in their lives.

He then explores the Bible to show how God's peace has a central theme in both the Old and New Testament. Plus, he points out that blessings should be in abundance for Christians.

Later, the writer shares how as a child he was separated from, his mum and dad at the age of 4. He openly shares that he had no peace as a child. Further he opens his heart to reveal that he has no recollection or any picture of his mum.

Later in life he lives with and cares for his dad. His dad told him not to look for his mum, although the writer wanted to. When his dad dies, he wrestles with the idea of looking for his mum. The writer's sister had tried but failed. He decides he has to find his mum. He longs to look into her eyes and just squeeze her tightly. However, the writer is in for a shock.

He then shares the blessings of having a Christian wife for the last 22 years plus, how God has given them two beautiful boys. He shares how becoming a Christian has not brought unity to his extended family. He puts this down to the completely different lifestyle he has now and has had for the last 26 years. Gone are the smoking, drinking and bad language that made him a hit with the family and old friends.

The theme running through the book is the writer's love for God. Plus he shows how God's perfect peace has directed his life thus far. There is a very strong testimony to the riches of Christ. He also asserts that the peace he has found, together with the special love of Jesus are available to all who would call on the beautiful name of Jesus.

-

God's Perfect Peace In Action

Official Disclaimer

Published by David J Portman
Printed by Leopard Press, Cradley Heath, West Midlands.

ISBN – 978-0-9555546-0-5

British Library Cataloguing-in-publication Data.
A catalogue record for this book is available from the British Library

C.I.P.

First printed 2007, second print 2008

God's Perfect Peace in Action

CONTENTS

My Genesis 1979

CHAPTER 1

In 1979 I was twenty-six years of age. I was single and living at home. I had a girlfriend who had been with me for three years. I had an Allegro, which was a super car. I was employed as a car seat trimmer, for which I was very grateful. The job paid very well. As I left school with only one certificate (and that was only for swimming one length of the baths) I was pleased to be employed. My school days were more about surviving than education! However, the job was good and my work colleagues were great. I had been a seat trimmer for some seven years; first starting in the cutting department then advancing to the trimming department. We built seats for Triumph, T.V.R and Jenson to name but a few of the car manufacturers.

My work colleagues and I had been talking one day about belief in God. I had said that I could not really say if I believed in God. My reason for that comment was, as I said to my friends, I didn't know God. However, things were about to change.

As I recall, I started to feel a little low in my life. There had been no major changes but I just felt low. I had plenty of money. The problem was that I was not really enjoying my life. One day I went to my bedroom, knelt down and asked God to reveal Himself to me. I prayed that if He was real then He could have my life. I told God He was welcome to it. The deal was He had to reveal Himself. I still remember getting up and just getting on with my life. I know I had no peace then in my heart. I tried to please other people and I was a bit of a perfectionist and a worried person.

Life went on. However, I did start to read a Christian article in the Sunday Mercury. The Minister told the readers how much God loved them and encouraged the readers to trust God more. I used to spend hours analysing his message. The message was a different language to me. How could I trust in someone I did not know? The Minister said I had to lose my life in order to find it! What kind of language is that! Further, he said Jesus had a fantastic life for me. All these thoughts and more were going round my head. For the first time in my life I was contemplating whether God existed or not!

One day at work, my thoughts turned to a baby. I was thinking about how babies are formed, their eyes, ears etc. I came to the conclusion that there had to be a designer at work, and this designer was God. I had found faith and it felt good. I can still remember the day; in a factory, people working round me, and me admitting to myself that God existed. Little did I know that there was much, much more of God to enter into my life.

All of a sudden my life was to change. The factory was to close in six months time. My colleagues and I were all going to be made redundant. This was not a very nice thought. What a shock! What was I going to do? Where was I going? Besides enjoying the work, my colleagues were also my main social friends. Some of them I drank with, some I holidayed with, and some I played five-a-side football with. Little did I know I was going to meet a new friend; His name was Jesus.

Meanwhile the Minister's messages were both complex and simple. The complex parts troubled me. How could God have really died for me? How did Jesus rise from that tomb? How did He talk to people in this new body? I was wrestling with all these points and more – I certainly had no peace.

However, the simple messages were very easy to understand. The Minister said that if we had a problem then we should take the problem to Jesus, and ask Him to solve it!

The Minister's article was called, "Lets face it." I was trying my hardest to face my problems. However, worry was getting the better of me, and I had no peace at all. Given my present situation, where my future looked bleak, I read these articles with great interest and finally started to pray! To my great surprise my request for a job was answered. Consequently, a month or so before the factory closed I secured my redundancy cheque and started a new job. The factory closed on the 6th June and I had already started my new job on May 1st. WOW!

My new situation was, I believed, the result of praying to Jesus. I should point out that some of my work friends took a dislike to me because they were all more qualified than me; one, in particular, was really nasty. I had beaten them to the new job. Little did they know Jesus was on my side. I started praying for other things and to my surprise my requests were answered. Clearly as it says in Genesis 1 verse 1, 'In the beginning God created the heavens and the earth.' He chose to truly bless me. God's wonderful peace was descending upon me and how majestic and refreshing it was. That was my Genesis story.

The Gospel

CHAPTER 2

This chapter is called the gospel. The gospel is really the name for "good news." I was about to hear the best news I have ever heard. Plus, this good news was going to touch me in a tremendous way. I was going to hear the gospel, accept the gospel and try and live my life in accordance with the gospel. In contrast, someone close to me was about to hear some sad news, which would break her heart.

As I have said, the Minister's article in the paper was both complex and simple. I knew no other Christians; therefore, I had to try and understand this deep message of Christianity all on my own. I found that a very difficult, hard and lonely thing to do.

I had been in my new job about six months. I worked in Birmingham as a seat trimmer. Some of the seats I trimmed I had worked on at the other factory. There were only a handful of workers and I was the only one who was experienced enough to trim some of the seats. This gave me confidence, and at this particular time, life was good. However, life was going to get much, much better! Out of the blue, God was about to touch my life in a deeper way.

My attention was drawn to a Cliff Richard Gospel concert. A girl at work, who was a Cliff fan, was sending for tickets and kindly requested a couple of tickets for me. The tickets arrived and I went with a friend to the concert. I was not really a Cliff fan, but the concert changed my direction in life, or, more accurately, it confirmed the way I wanted to go. I remember being at the concert, listening to Cliff's words, seeing all the people there. I knew I wanted more of Jesus in my life. The Gospel, the good news, was really touching my life and starting to change it. Cliff's words about Jesus were like a magnet to my heart. I wanted to collect all his thoughts and just let them wash over me! Looking at the people there, they all looked alive and excited. I started to think; "Does Jesus excite other people like He excites me?" I knew the answer was "Yes" because I could see it on people's faces.

I have to mention that the girl who got the tickets for me totally disliked the concert. She expected all his hits, not his gospel songs. The friend whom I took with me was, in fact, my fiancée. It was a sad time for her; she obviously knew I had changed my approach to life and now she witnessed Birmingham Town Hall being full of 'crazy' people just like me! I can recall that with any problems we had, my answer was always the same; "Jesus will sort it out." Looking back, it must have been very hard for her. However, I was full of Jesus' love. I knew I wanted more of Him.

The excitement He gave me was incredible. His peace was unbelievable. I was receiving feelings that I had never experienced before. I desired to meet more Christians like the ones I saw at the concert. I also wanted to find a church. The need I had to go to church was tremendous. However, my fiancée had no such feelings. We had been together for four years. I was very much part of her family and they accepted me like a family member. My fiancée and I were very close, but all that was about to change!

The Parting of the Ways

CHAPTER 3

I recall that after the Cliff concert my faith deepened. I had been encouraged in my faith in a tremendous way. The Gospel concert and the way I felt inside were two sides of the same coin. I could relate to much of what Cliff had said about Jesus. Added to this, I felt at one with the audience. I can see it in my mind's eye; the audience contained very young and old folk and even nuns, and they all had this energy, love, peace in their eyes. It was fantastic! But what of my fiancée? She thought I was very strange. I had received this new peace in my life, and in any given situation I would say, "God will deal with the problem." Was it getting too much for her?

God's peace is wonderful, but sometimes this peace does bring unrest in friendships and family life. I remember that my desire to go to church was like a hunger. This hunger kept getting greater and greater. We went to a wedding service and being in church was fantastic! Once again, I was on a tremendously emotional high.

I had very little biblical teaching. I did go to Sunday school as a child but I never received any teaching which was as dynamic as I had found Jesus to be. I had mainly found adult people quite strange, saying one thing and doing another. One Sunday I did pop into a church but it seemed so dull and boring. I was adamant that they hadn't got the Jesus I knew. I was not free to choose because of my relationship with my fiancée. What I was free to do was pray! No one could stop me doing this; no one could get in my way when I was talking to God privately. As I recall, the Minister always encouraged me to pray. His faith was tremendous and he encouraged me greatly. So the time came to pray about my present situation.

My prayer was simple; I just wanted God to tell me what to do! Should I stay with my fiancée and honour and respect our relationship? I can still remember the night I prayed. This girl had meant so much to me. She was the first girl I had dated. She was so beautiful and had a great personality. We had shared our lives together for so long. However, we were going in different ways now. I had met Jesus and I was looking for a different direction in life to that of my girlfriend.

The prayer went something like this; "Jesus I need your direction in my life. I feel totally confused with my girlfriend. Should I stay with her, hoping that she will find you? Or should I depart from her and seek the new life you have for me? Please answer my prayer. I need to hear your voice. Amen and thank you Jesus"

To my utter surprise, I was woken up in the middle of the night and a voice said to me "Depart from her." The next day I clearly remembered the voice. But what should I do? We had been together for five years and were planning on being together all our lives. I hadn't got the courage to tell my fiancée that our friendship was over. I told myself that logically the voice was just me having a bad dream because I had things on my mind. However, within a very short time God's will was done.

I called for my fiancée and there was a strange feeling in the room. All her family were quiet and seemed on edge. We went out for a drive, and then she told me that our engagement was over. She said I had changed so much that I was a different person and she could not relate to me anymore. She was so upset and crying quite a lot. I was shocked but the peace I received was unbelievable. I knew that God had had his way, even though I had not been faithful to His message. I had been weak by not obeying what God had told me to do.

We are in the year 1981; February, to be precise. I am a Christian but know no other Christian people. I am alone, and a little lonely, if I am truthful, but I know I want more of Jesus in my life. I had His peace to stabilise me. My life was soon to change again! I was going to be made redundant again, but this time the 'new creature' was more prepared for it, and really half expected it. I had a feeling that God had something new for me to do. I saw redundancy as this calling or direction to me. The door of life was opening for me, but where would it lead me?

New Creation in Christ

CHAPTER **4**

The Bible teaches us that we are a new creation in Christ Jesus (2Cor 5:17). What a fantastic statement that is whether we are seven or seventy. I felt a new creature when I first met Jesus and twenty-seven years later I'm still feeling new. For me God's peace is the driving force. I never realised that God could give us so much. As a child I thought religion was just like any other subject one had to learn. I never realised the riches that we have in Christ. It is interesting to note that in John 14 Jesus tells His disciples to receive His peace. This event took place before the coming of the Holy Spirit. Jesus' nature is to give. He gave when He walked on the earth. Thankfully, He still gives today. His peace for me is the most important aspect of His love. Yes, He forgives, but for me the proof of His existence is by way of the peace He gives.

In John 14:27 Jesus said "Peace, I leave with you." What a blessing for the disciples! No doubt we have all lost loved ones or friends, and they have left us some word or thought or style of life. However, to receive this gift from Jesus must have been so wonderful. Further, Jesus says "My peace I give you"(John 14:27). If a friend buys us a gift it is a joy, but to receive Jesus' peace - what beautiful words! It's worth noting this was all said before the Holy Spirit had descended on the believers.

The general giving of the Holy Spirit guarantees the peace of Jesus (Gal 5:22) to all believers. No wonder that it is a tremendous experience at the time of conversion; one is changed from the world's experiences and strife to the calmness of Jesus' peace. What a gift we can all receive from Jesus.

When we look at the life of Saul, we see clear evidence of strife, as he was hunting down Christians. Later in his life we see the effect of Jesus because he had received God's peace. To the Romans, Paul states "Therefore, since we have been justified through faith, we have peace with God through our Lord Jesus Christ." (Rom 5:1) Once the human heart meets its maker the circuit is complete, the light of Jesus shines, and peace is a resident in the body. Paul reiterates his message in Romans 14:17 where he makes reference to peace. Here he states "For the Kingdom of God is not a matter of eating and drinking, but of righteousness, peace and joy in the Holy Spirit," Clearly Paul is saying 'Don't be robbed or cheated but seek the fullness of God.'

When the great debate in Galatia erupted Paul reasserts the same message. He tells the Galatians that the fruit of the spirit is love, joy, and peace... (Gal 5:22). When babies are born they take on the surname of their parents. Likewise, when Christians are born they take on what God has for them. A baby has that name for life; I believe we have God's peace for at least this life. No wonder the writer affirms to the Ephesians that, "For he himself is our peace..."(Eph 2:14). What a wonderful statement then and so true and wonderful today.

In 1981 I was going to be made redundant, but this time the 'new creature' was more prepared for it, and even half expected it. I had a feeling that God had something new for me to do. I saw redundancy as His direction for me. The only problem for me was that I did not know what it was going to be!

Training for the Future

CHAPTER 5

In early 1981, I found myself without a job, single, no Christian friends and not knowing what the future held. However the one thing I was certain about was that Jesus loved me and cared for me. I knew that Jesus had a plan for me and that He was my lovely Saviour. I was really having a fantastic time relaxing and preparing for what Christ had in store for me. I had an inner feeling that I needed to improve my education. Consequently, when September came I enrolled on 'O' Level Courses at Warley College. I went to Warley College because I tried to enrol on a Leisure and Recreation Course; however the entrance qualifications were too high for me. The course tutor was super; he suggested I complete 'O' Level English, Maths and Sociology, then move on to the Leisure and Recreation Course the following year. I thought this was sound advice.

Being a mature student was humbling and nervous at times. I hadn't studied before; I hadn't even read a book until I became a Christian. I needed to work hard on all aspects of education. This I did with a tremendous amount of enthusiasm. However the positive side at college outweighed the negative side. College life was fantastic. I soon made friends, both boys and girls. My English teacher was a super lady. She said I could be her teacher's pet! This had never happened at school. I felt so good at college. I mixed well with the students in the gym and the puddings in the refectory were fantastic! My academic progress was good; I just wanted to learn so much. I couldn't stop reading or writing or asking questions. I soon read all the relevant books and had lots of information in my head.

My major obstacle was writing all the details down. I was way too slow! To put this right I would practise writing answers in forty minutes, with ten minutes rest in between. I would do three answers per night. After a few nights my speed was there. It was also a good way to revise.

When the time came for the tutors to submit names for the examination I was a borderline case. In Sociology my friend, a fellow student aged about sixteen years old, persuaded the tutor to put my name forward for the 'O' Level Paper. In English, I was going to sit the Stage One Paper. The reason for this was that the English teacher wanted me to end the year with some qualification, even if it was a lower certificate. However, at the examination time, I sat a higher Paper in English because of a mistake by the college. It was good for me because I passed the Stage Three Paper, which I was told was just below 'A' level. Added to this, I gained O Level Sociology Grade C. I did various sports courses during the year. My hard work was rewarded with quite a few certificates in total plus a special gift from the college for the most improved student for that particular year. Furthermore, I was offered a place on the Leisure and Recreation Course, which was for a City and Guilds Certificate. I was really pleased and knew that God had blessed the work I had done.

About this time a leaflet came through the letter-box and once again my life was about to be drastically changed. The leaflet was advertising a Tent Crusade in Netherton. It was actually on the playing fields of my old Secondary School. I felt good about the idea and was hoping and praying that I would meet Christian people who thought like me. Up until then I had only been reading the Christian newspaper articles and watching 'Songs of Praise'. Both were very good, but I knew I needed more. The meetings were on every evening for a week.

I only missed one night which was because I had tickets with my family for a football match. The meetings were fantastic. The preacher talked about the Jesus I knew, the one that is alive and is always ready to meet our need. Also, the Christian people were very friendly. When the meetings finished I was invited to attend a series of meetings in a local church in Netherton. The first night I was given a Bible. When I went home I started to read it. As I read the New Testament I was filled with joy and tears. To read how much God loved me and to know all the things He had done for me was quite remarkable.

I was soon invited to visit another local church and very quickly became part of the fellowship. My diary went like this; Mondays, Boys' Club; Wednesdays, Prayer Meetings and Bible Study; Fridays Youth Meetings; Sundays, Morning and Evening Services and Sunday school in the afternoon. I loved the church and all the activities. I also met Irene at Primrose Hill Congregational Church. She was busy at the time studying and she would later receive her Bachelor of Education degree.

It is fantastic when God touches us and changes us for the better and then releases us to do His will and receive maximum fulfilment in life. Again, for me, God's driving force is His peace.

Meanwhile, the Leisure and Recreation Course was going really well. It was one of the best twelve months I have known and certainly the best course I have ever attended. I absolutely loved the course which had academic study in the morning and sport every afternoon. I have always enjoyed sport but at school the teaching I felt was poor and communication was dire. To my surprise I found that I was good at most sports. I certainly had found a new confidence, and having stopped smoking and drinking I had lots more energy and stamina.

The reason I stopped drinking was because I found I could enjoy myself better without alcohol. One day I remember, some friends and I went to a party. I was driving, so therefore, I only drank pop. To my surprise, I didn't miss the alcohol, and, in fact, found that God's presence was more than enough to give me enjoyment and satisfy me.

The course taught me so much and took me to lots of sporting places. I did a project on football violence and to enhance the project I interviewed the Aston Villa Manager. All the staff and fellow students knew about my faith and respected me wonderfully well. I had to finance myself for twelve months because I couldn't get a grant, but that was no great sacrifice. God always provides all we need; we just have to ask and to have the faith to believe. Psalm 23 is a great example of this; the Lord is our Shepherd and He provides daily for our needs. Psalm 23 never mentions peace but surely peace underpins the whole Psalm.

Before the Leisure and Recreation Course finished I knew where I wanted to go next; a Bible College. Finally, the course came to an end; it had been a wonderful experience. I had gained a City and Guilds Certificate in Leisure and Recreation Management as well as other sporting qualifications. However, my only real achievement was that I had trusted in Jesus and His wonderful will for my life. After the Leisure and Recreation Course, I really felt a desire to go to Bible College. I couldn't go far because I was caring for my dad who was actually housebound. However, God always provides.

At my local church we had speakers from Birmingham Bible Institute; they always had a good message and were very encouraging people. My thirst for knowledge and, in particular, the Bible was incredible. I wanted to know all about the Bible, the people in it and especially about Jesus. Therefore, I decided to enrol at Birmingham Bible Institute. I was so excited about studying there.

Irene decided that she believed it was also right to go to BBI; she had a grant for two years and was a residential student. I decided to travel in and pay term by term. Unfortunately, on the Saturday night, which was the induction course night, while the service continued I had no peace at all about the college. Irene felt really at home with the college, but I didn't. I struggled on for one term but then left. It just didn't seem right. There were students there from all over the world; some with certain problems and they needed help. The academic part of the college was not really to my liking, since I wanted more intense studying. I felt sad but strong inside with God's peace. Verses like Romans 8:28 "And we know that in all things God works for the good for those who love him, who have been called according to his purpose," are a great comfort at difficult times. Irene had a fantastic two years; I had to wait and see what God had for me.

I started listening to lots of Bible tapes by a Bible teacher named Roger Price. The tapes were fantastic and just what I wanted. There was a series of Basic Bible Tapes, plus other tapes on specific topics like death, heaven etc. I must have listened to about one hundred tapes. The tapes bedded in my faith.

However, I soon got a job working in a Leisure Centre - well I had some training for it! The job was four evenings a week, therefore I had the days free. The thirst to study was as strong as ever so I looked at 'A' Levels at colleges. I think it was Irene who suggested I study for 'A' level Religious Studies. I went along to Halesowen College and enrolled for 'A' level Religious Studies and Sociology. My RS teacher thought I was a little strange and didn't have much faith in me academically. He was a lovely Christian man who had started work as a miner and later had met the Risen Jesus. I think I was a little bit too lively for him. The RS course was good. I studied issues like war, peace, existence of God and books in the Bible. I loved it and to my surprise I found it quite easy. Sociology was good too; it's about the study of people in society.

My RS teacher was pleased with the examination result I achieved - a 'B' grade. My Sociology teacher was super; very supportive and encouraging. I achieved a 'C' grade in Sociology. Jesus had truly blessed and guided me again by His wonderful peace.

After 'A' levels I was so excited and encouraged to study more. I decided to enquire about the possibility of studying at University. I certainly had the desire and thirst to study more. If I could study for a degree in theology then I was going to try my best to secure a place at Birmingham University.
After the initial interviews, I was invited to attend the evening classes for two years then change to daytime study. My evening classes, which were three times a week, seven until nine, counted for a full year. After that I would have to attend daytime lectures for a further two years. At the completion of the course was a BA Honours degree in Theology.

I loved University. It was fantastic! I was based at Edgbaston and Selly Oak. My studies included New Testament Greek, Old Testament and New Testament Studies, Sociology, Early Christian Theology, Islam, Judaism and other similar topics.

I did a dissertation on Dietrich Bonhoeffer, who was a German theologian.
I also did a ten thousand word Paper on C. T. Russell, the founder of the Jehovah's Witnesses. Early church history was exciting to study. So, too, was Judaism. I was fascinated with the holocaust theology. Some Jews lost their faith at this terrible time, while others fasted for the special festival times, even though they were being starved to death!

At University they had super sports facilities, and with also cycling about sixteen miles per day, I was keeping fit in both my head and my body. God richly blessed my time at University. In many ways it has left a lasting effect on me.

Looking back I feel I was in awe of the lecturers. However, they did help me grow as a person in many ways. Most of them were very kind and very humble people. I felt God's peace with me as I studied and especially with all those final examinations! With God's help, I managed to obtain an honours degree in theology which was a fantastic result for me.

Having gained the degree I had to think and pray about my next project. All through my studies, at the back of mind, I was always trying to find the will of God. Ephesians 2:8-10 states "For it is by grace you have been saved, through faith and this not from yourself, it is the gift of God - not by works, so that no-one can boast. For we are God's workmanship, created in Christ Jesus to do good works, which God prepared in advance for us to do." What I desired was to know for myself 'the good works' that God had prepared for me. I had been a Christian for about eleven years now; I was still no nearer to finding God's will for my life. However, I believed I was on the right pathway and I was certainly having fun.

Study wise, my next step was to train to be a Religious Teacher and to enrol on a PGCE Course. I chose this because I wanted to use my degree and it seemed right. The course never seemed good. My fellow students, in the main, were a little snobbish and the course was very cliquey. I completed my teaching practice, having taught in three different schools. However, I never applied for a teaching post, because I never thought it was quite right for me. I think at the back of my mind I wanted to have a job which was church-based. One thing I did know; I believed that my studies had come to an end, and that I had to wait for Jesus to reveal what he had for me. I wanted Ephesians 2:8-10 to be fulfilled. Was I asking for too much? Should I settle for an ordinary job? What really did the future hold for me in an employment sense?

The Ministry Arrives

CHAPTER 6

Before I was a Christian I had had three jobs in eleven years. In contrast, the first fourteen years of being a Christian saw me having numerous jobs. These jobs included: community play leader, shop assistant, taxi driver, sports hall assistant, self-employed window cleaner, warehouse worker, upholsterer, car seat trimmer and working with young people with learning difficulties. Some of the jobs were part-time. A few of the jobs started part-time, but then I was offered full-time posts. Always I kept looking for that special job. Most of the jobs were good. Working as a community play leader was interesting. This was a summer job. I would travel round Sandwell visiting different parks and organising sporting activities. Great Barr was super but other areas were more challenging and could be a little dangerous. For instance, in Victoria Park, Tipton, I had a group of young boys who had been glue sniffing. That situation could have turned nasty. In Wednesbury, at Friar Park, I was fielding in a cricket match, just standing there, and a dog came and wee'ed up my leg! Such is life! The other jobs just came and went; usually, they just fitted in with my studies and seasonal jobs.

How do we find a job that best fits our gifts or do we just do it for the money? Well I'm not a money-orientated person, so it had to be for the gifts. Quite a few people would say to me, "What are you going to do with all those certificates?" Truthfully, I had no idea! I just completely trusted Jesus to direct me. Some of my family members took a dislike to my studying but I just carried on. I have to say some people in church thought I was a little strange too! I knew I was doing God's will so I was strong in my faith, even if I was a little frustrated.

After University I knew I had to put a full stop to the studies and concentrate on looking for employment. Someone mentioned that I contact a church vocational advisor. This turned out to be a super idea. Her name was Linda Woolhouse, a Christian. She informed me that there was a job at a nearby church in Oldswinford and she encouraged me to apply for it. The job was working alongside the Minister. If I thought it was right I had to move and live in a flat on-site that the church provided. We are in 1993. In 1990, sadly, my dad died. If we moved, it meant Irene, Josh and I had to make a big commitment! We decided it was the right thing to do. I had great peace and excitement about it. St Mary's Oldswinford was soon to be our new home. I had only ever had two homes in forty years, so Jesus was moving me on as he did with the jobs.

The Minister was supportive towards me. He was sympathetic to God's calling on my life. He encouraged me to apply for the Ministry and to become a vicar, if I thought it was right. After certain interviews I didn't think it was right. The job at St Mary's was good and taught me lots of things. It built up my confidence and I felt well supported with the church team at St Mary's. However, it still didn't seem a fulfilment of Eph 2:10.

Then one day I had a phone call from an old maths tutor. He asked me if I could teach a boy English at the boy's home. After giving it some thought I said yes. I went to the boy's home, gave him his lesson, and really enjoyed it. Immediately, I believed this was what God wanted me to do. Some thirteen years on, I still do the same job and believe, and tell people, it is a gift from God. I started teaching English to that ten-year-old boy. Since then I have taught from pre-school to G.C.S.E. and mature students. I teach Maths, English and Science from pre-school to G.C.S.E.

I also help with revising, if pupils require that. The only rule I have in the lesson is not to worry. This is what Jesus tells me to do in Matthew's Gospel 6:25f and I pass it on to the pupils. The pupil's reaction is fantastic, because it relaxes them so much and I get the best out of them. I have a waiting list for pupils who want me to teach them – it's great! To find God's will for our lives is, I believe, the most important aspect of one's life.

The job is very fulfilling. In one case I taught two sisters, who had twelve months difference in age, and both gained entrance to King Edward's schools. At present, I am teaching a boy aged seven and he has difficulty in basic Maths and English. He is improving greatly; his mother says when I leave he is on a terrific high. Another boy I taught had difficulty in remembering things, or so his mum thought. After a couple of lessons I told his mum he did not have a problem. At the time the boy was eight and not doing very well at school. When he was in year 11 the school wanted to enter him for G.C.S.E. high level English and Maths. Added to this, the pupil started a very successful sporting career. The special needs cases are very rewarding when you see the pupils advance. This is usually because I give them a massive amount of encouragement and I find out what motivates them.

I thank God daily for the job. I say job but it's really a hobby, I'm really still studying myself. The peace I receive from tutoring is unbelievable. I also see the pupils improve and that is a great reward. The journey to the job was incredible and the job itself is fantastic.

I believe God has so much for each one of us; we just have to ask, have faith and just wait for His timing. Also we should not wait until we are at 'death's door' to ask Him because He so desires to bless us now.

Is My Story Biblical?

CHAPTER 7

From time to time we hear people state how their lives have changed. My life has changed and I would like to show that the change is similar to events that the Bible records.

I have mentioned John 14, where Jesus said, "My peace I give you" In John 14:27, Jesus said "Peace I leave with you." The Apostle Paul talked about peace in Galatians 5:22 and Romans 14:17. I believe that Paul, after the Damascus Road incident, found a new quality of peace. That peace he would attribute to God. The change that he and others portray in the New Testament is quite remarkable. As you will recall, Paul persecuted the Christians. We are told in Acts that Paul was actually at the stoning of Stephen. Later, Paul would preach the same message as Stephen. And like Stephen, Paul would give the ultimate sacrifice; namely his own life.

In this chapter I am trying to lay a biblical foundation and state that the peace I am personally referring to is the same peace that is mentioned in the New Testament. This peace is from God and life changing. It arrives when a person has a personal encounter with Christ.

In John's Gospel (Ch 3), Jesus has a conversation with Nicodemus. Jesus tells him that a person has to have a life-changing experience in order to see the kingdom of God. Later, in Ch 4, Jesus tells the Samaritan woman that whoever takes 'water' from Him would never be thirsty again. In Ch 6, Jesus declared, "I am the bread of life. He who comes to me will never go hungry and he who believes in me will never be thirsty." Clearly these passages are open for interpretation; to me they show that belief in Jesus brings forth peace and contentment.

In Luke's Gospel Ch 15, there is a whole chapter referring to the lost sheep, lost coin, and the famous story about the lost son. At the end of each story there is rejoicing when the lost item is found. Obviously the 'item' in each story relates to, or is a mirror image of, how God feels when a person turns to Him.
History portrays an abundance of people who have had a similar experience to me. People who had a personal encounter with Christ started the early church and through the years the pattern has continued.

When we look in the Old Testament there are many references to peace. In Leviticus 26:6, "I will grant peace in the land..." This was a reward for obedience. The passage goes on to say, (verse 9-13) "I will look on you with favour and make you fruitful and increase your numbers and I will keep my covenant with you. You will still be eating last year's harvest when you will have to move it out to make room for the new. I will put my dwelling place among you, and I will not abhor you .I will walk among you and be your God, and you will be my people... I broke the bars of your yoke and enabled you to walk with heads held high." So many things there that God promised to do for His people. He promised to show favour and to make them fruitful. This is about all aspects of God being in touch with His people. The passage has no tone of God being distant; on the contrary, He is walking side by side with His people. I like the part which refers to the breaking of their yokes. It brings forth pictures of cows being held by yokes, and then, suddenly, being set free to roam and enjoy life. In my view, this is a picture of what God can do for us.

In Numbers 6:22-26 we have the priestly blessing: "The Lord said to Moses 'tell Aaron and his sons, this is how you are to bless the Israelites. Say to them, the Lord bless you and keep you, the Lord make His face shine upon you and be gracious to you, the Lord turn His face towards you and give you peace'." It's worth noting this blessing is still said in some churches today.

When we move onto 1Kings 2:33 it states, "...But on David and his descendants, his house and his throne, may there be the Lord's peace for ever." What a wonderful thought - the Lord's peace forever!

Moving on to the Psalms, those wonderful songs to God, we find in Psalm 29:11 "The Lord gives strength to His people, the Lord blesses His people with peace." In the long Psalm of 119 we find in verse 165, "Great peace have they who love your law and nothing can make them stumble."

In Proverbs 14:30, we find reference to peace: "A heart at peace gives life to the body, but envy rots the bones." That great chapter 9 in Isaiah which many connect to the prophecy to Jesus states in verse 6, "For to us a child is born, to us a son is given, and the government will be on His shoulders . And He will be called Wonderful Counsellor, Mighty God, Everlasting Father, Prince Of Peace." Later, in Isaiah 32:17, "The fruit of righteousness will be peace..." This clearly has echoes of Galatians 5:22 in the New Testament.

The Suffering Servant passage in Isaiah 52:13 – 53 which many scholars believe relates to Jesus' suffering on the cross mentions this glorious peace too. In Isaiah 53:5: "But he was pierced for our transgressions, he was crushed for our iniquities; the punishment that brought us peace was upon him and by his wounds we are healed." This really is a fantastic passage; it contains, for me, the prophecy of Jesus' sacrifice for us all. It goes into great detail. The cost of it is depicted many years later in the Mel Gibson movie, "The Passion of the Christ!" The passage is really worth reading; it tells of how Christ gave of Himself; how He was speared; how He was silent; how He was led to be killed; how He was innocent; and how the servant brings us closer to God the Father.

Later, in Isaiah 54:10, the writer places God's love alongside His peace - what a beautiful combination. Here is the verse, "Though the mountains be shaken and the hills be removed, yet my unfailing love for you will not be shaken nor my covenant of peace be removed." What a lovely promise.

Ezekiel 34:25,26 states that God will make an agreement of love with His people, "I will make a covenant of peace with them... I will bless them.... there will be showers of blessings." Again these verses display a God who is close to His people and not distant at all. Ezekiel 37:26 states, "I will make a covenant of peace with them, it will be an everlasting covenant..." Here the agreement or covenant of peace is repeated, and it is asserted that the 'deal' is everlasting. Not many things last forever but God promises His peace will last forever; what a promise!

Even in the last book of the Old Testament, in Malachi 2:5, we find, "My covenant was with him a covenant of life and peace..." Clearly a thread can be seen through the Old Testament relating to God's peace and His people.

Why Choose Peace? Why is it Important?

CHAPTER **8**

If another Christian were to write a similar book, they could choose a different theme which is precious to them. He or she could, for example, choose forgiveness. The Bible teaches us that God forgives; therefore, if a person has done a terrible act then to be forgiven by God would be special to them. Likewise, if a person has not been shown much love in life and suddenly finds out how much God loves them and how much love He has for them, then it will have a profound effect on the person. I should mention if he or she has been bound or addicted to a drug, or a pattern of life stops, and they have found the freedom that Christ brings, then, obviously the aspect of being free in life would be their main theme of God. So, why have I chosen peace? Did I have a life of torment before I became a Christian?

Firstly, before I answer those questions, I have to make a general comment. God's peace is very special to all Christians and unique. Peace is a gift to all believers, given by God. However, for me personally, it is a double blessing. When I was very young, aged about four, my mum and dad separated. Consequently, I was separated from my parents. My eldest sister, some nine years older than me, went to live in a children's home. My other sister, who is two years older than me, was cared for, as I was, by my auntie and uncle. We saw our dad about twice a week, but I was never at ease with him in those days (though later came to love him in a special way). As for my mum, I never saw her again. I can't remember what she looked like. I do have a good memory for faces but at the age of three I think this skill was just developing. I never saw my mum through my school days.

In fact, no contact has ever been made with my mum since I was three.

My dad would always say that I was better not knowing her at all. He told me this as a child and as an adult. Obviously, she may have seen me. She knew where I lived. Sometimes I would stare at strange women and wonder if they were my mum. This would happen at the school gates, in the street or round the shops. Well, if she was there, she never came to me. I would really love to see a picture of her but up until now I have never seen her face. However, not wanting to upset dad I never tried to find her.

Sadly, in 1990, my dad died and after a time of contemplation, I decided to search for my mum. I must admit I was very nervous and excited about finding mum. To my surprise, I was soon close to finding her. I spoke to her brother, my uncle, who lived some one hundred and forty miles away. He told me that she had been living some twelve miles away from my home. Furthermore, as we chatted, I found out that she had been on the Isle of Wight for a holiday at the same time that I had been on the island. I may have walked past her in the street. What a thought! The sad news that he gave me was that she, like my dad, had also passed away. She had died a few years before my dad. I went one day to the town where she lived. That was very strange, knowing that mum had walked and shopped where I was actually walking now. I had her death certificate so I walked past where she lived, and that was a strange experience.

Because of my childhood, I can say that I never knew peace and contentment until I gave my heart to Jesus. As for love, how do we define that? I would sometimes watch my auntie with her son and see the love she had for him, which was only right. But, at the same time, I knew no-one loved me that much. As a young boy, growing up in someone else's home, I was utterly grateful and still am. Bitterness has never been part of my thinking.

Nevertheless, I always compare my childhood to like living in a hotel. Hotels are great but they aren't home. The embarrassment I had through not having a mum and dad around was very uncomfortable to live with. Divorce was not fashionable in the 1960's! My friends would ask me why I lived with my auntie and uncle but I never had an answer. I was always too shy to say. I have spoken to one of my primary school teachers and she said I was very unsettled at school. I know that my local doctor felt sorry for me because of the unhappiness in my early years. Peace played no part in my life really until I was twenty-six years old.

When I asked God to make my life better and answer my prayers, a wonderful peace came upon me! What a tremendous God we have. Twenty-eight years on and the peace is still as wonderful. And God is still answering my prayers. My childhood was good. I am not the kind of person to be bitter or angry. I would have loved a mum and dad at home. What child would not? However, my childhood was good. I will always be grateful to my auntie and uncle and cousin for offering my sister and I a home. I received an abundance of things from God when I became a Christian; for me, the most important was peace inside my heart.

God's Peace in the Family

CHAPTER **9**

Everyone who holds family life dear to their hearts would desire peace in their family. I have to smile when people say 'Join this group', and they add, 'We are just like a family.' I smile, because most families, I would suggest, have conflicts and fallouts.

I have observed it is usually the mum or dad who are the hub of the family. They usually keep the family together. Once mum and dad die then families can splinter. However, how has God affected my family life and me?
When I became a Christian I was living with my dad, just the two of us at home. Dad would have been sixty-six when I became a Christian. Sadly, when dad was sixty-five years old and just a week before he was about to retire, he suddenly went almost blind. One tea-time he said that his eyes were going dark. I can picture him now in my mind's eye. He was scared, terrified and in shock because his vision was going. I took dad to the eye hospital. After a few days investigation the doctors believed that dad had a blood clot or his arteries were just furring up. He was finally classified as partially sighted. He never liked this phrase because he said he couldn't see!

With dad being in this position I really got to know him very well and we built a strong relationship. Previously, when I was younger and living with my aunt and uncle, dad was almost a stranger. I had in fact been living with dad for about 3 years. In 1976 my sister persuaded me to move and live with her and dad. As you will recall at the age of about four I went to live with my aunt, uncle and cousin. Unfortunately, my cousin died of an enlarged heart at the age of 26. The following year my auntie died after a series of heart attacks.

This left my uncle and I together. We had a good relationship. We both liked sport and both drank in the local public house. The only problem was that I had found a girlfriend (later to be my fiancée).

My uncle introduced a new rule; the rule was I had to be back home at 12:00! Bear in mind that I was twenty three! If I was back home after 12 I was locked out. Many Saturday nights I returned home, found the door bolted and slept in my car. The strange thing was when I entered the house in the morning we both chatted as if nothing had happened. When my sister heard about the situation she wanted me to leave my uncle and move in with her and my dad. Reluctantly I moved. It had been my home for some twenty years.

I never fell out with my uncle; I would visit him to see how he was. He was also invited to my wedding. I also shared the gospel with him many times. However, living with dad was a new experience. We were never close when I was a young boy and my sister was his favourite. Looking back, we were not very similar, I loved sport; he didn't. I liked to joke and have fun; he didn't. He was a serious man. However, with dad's illness and my becoming a Christian we grew close to each other. It is amazing how God breaks us down in certain areas and how His love can wash over us.

Dad always believed he was a Christian because he had been brought up in a Christian home. He had no idea of the personal relationship that can be had with Jesus. Dad only planned on me being at home for a short time. In fact he encouraged me to buy a property. After a while, when he got to know me, he asked me to stay with him. Our friendship grew and grew. I would read a passage of scripture to dad most nights. His favourite was Jonah and the fish. Dad and

I would also have a prayer time. Irene and I also took dad to a Billy Graham Crusade. On leaving the meeting he said he was very confused. He looked confused, but at least he now had ideas other than the one he was taught; namely he was born a Christian. The Bible doesn't teach this belief.

I would share my faith with dad whenever I could, and he would always accept what I said. On Sundays we would all go to church. He knew quite a few at the local church and obviously he heard the same message about Jesus there. God's peace and joy was in our home; it was fantastic. Dad would go and stay with my sisters some weekends but they became fewer and fewer since he preferred to stay at home.

When I met Irene dad made her very welcome. Irene and I discussed the future and particularly the part dad would play in it. We both knew that I had to care for my dad. It was my privilege to care for and to love my dad. I never knew my mum but I certainly knew my dad.

Within a week of meeting Irene I asked her to marry me. Unfortunately, she kept me waiting for a few months! She finally said 'Yes' when we were visiting her brother in Halifax. We were on the escalator in Asda and she said, 'Yes'. I was so pleased and grateful to God that I had found the girl of my dreams. The marriage service went really well with lots of Christian friends taking part. My best man gave a sermon that was very challenging and related to how Jesus suffered on the cross. It was a fantastic day. We have been married some twenty two years, but it only seems like two. Jesus has always been at the centre of our marriage. When we have problems we give them to Him. I am not an argumentative person by nature. I don't want any other woman so thankfully harmony is in our marriage. We both work together in the same direction in the home so I think this helps enormously. Added to that, we love each other dearly and we know God loves us both.

Sometimes it was difficult looking after dad. The last few years of his life he was almost confined to his bedroom, but God still blessed us greatly in abundance. We were offered a rotation bed at a local rest home. Dad would go in the rest home once every six weeks, thus giving Irene and I two weeks together. Obviously, I would still visit dad on daily basis. God is so true to his word. All things do work to the good for those who love Him. He gives us strength to cope with different situations. My love for dad when he was alive was precious. We were great together. About a week before he died, his mind started to drift, and he was saying strange things. However, God's peace inside me calmed dad down and gave him peace too. When he died, in 1990, through old age I was so upset. I wanted to move house to live close to his grave. I kept crying lots. Irene told me to stop and I did in public. But I would go upstairs and have a private cry on my own.

The feeling of being an orphan hit me hard. I can still remember where I was when I realised I was an orphan – no mum and no dad! It was strange because dad could hardly walk, see only a little, was very frail but at the same time he gave me enormous strength, love and confidence. His favourite saying to me was, "stay with me, David, I love your company." Then he would hold my hand and I just knew he was content and happy.

My own personal strength in God was strong at this sad time. I believe at times like these you have to put your life in overdrive or auto, and just do the things in life that get you by. Plus, Irene was a great support at this time. Now there were just the two of us plus a small dog named Rusty. I am so blessed to have a wife with such a strong faith who enjoys being very committed to Jesus. In 1990, when dad fell asleep, Irene had just gained her B.Ed degree and I had gained a BA in theology. She soon found a teaching post and started on a career that she loves. On the other hand, I was searching for God's will in my life. We were both very involved with church life, Youth For Christ and Christian holidays like Spring Harvest. God certainly does give us an abundant life if we try and receive from Him all the things He has planned for us.

Our thoughts soon turned to whether we should start a family or not. My view was that life was great as it was, but if Irene wanted a family I would not object. I'm so glad we decided to start a family. I can recall we went to Minehead; probably for Spring Harvest. We had a fantastic time. I remember playing tennis with Irene; she looked beautiful so radiant. On our return from Minehead Irene's pregnancy was confirmed. The countdown was now on for the arrival of the baby. We both went to parent classes and these helped greatly. However, I did feel both excited and nervous. I was excited about the birth of a new person, but nervous about the responsibility of being a father. Irene had a difficult time giving birth with some 21 hours in labour. Finally, when the baby arrived he looked fantastic. It was so exciting when we checked the baby for two eyes, ten fingers, ten toes and two ears etc.

I personally like to register the birth. It is a fantastic feeling to register a new life. The potential in a life is fantastic. We soon knew we had a baby since life changed completely! I truly do believe a baby is a gift from God. A baby is an unbelievably wonderful work; a treasure from God. For me, children are a clear statement that He exists.

The joys of being a parent are fantastic. However, it is or can be a very tiring job. We both needed God's strength and peace in looking after Josh. He was, and still is, a very active boy. I looked after Josh in the day and then went to work in the evening. This was extremely difficult, but as a parent you just do it. We love our children greatly but God loves us even more. What a thought! We would have some lovely days together. I fitted a child seat to my cycle and Josh and I would visit the local canal and feed the ducks, and then visit the local park and try and conquer the climbing frame! Obviously, we would finish with a picnic.

By nature I am a friendly person. I do not like confrontation. However, like most parents you do what you can for your child. Personal feelings go to one side – you just stand up for your child. For instance, when Josh started school the school was very poor in certain areas. I commented on these areas to the school and obviously this got me disliked. Later, I became a school governor in the same school and this was a challenging situation. Once again I turned to God for His guidance and His peace.

In 2000, our second son arrived, and I was still tired from looking after Josh. Thankfully, James is so placid and calm and has truly refreshed me. James tells us all the time how much he loves us. He went to a Christian playgroup and settled in really well. Later, he moved to a school nursery and then joined the school.

I love being a parent; being at home with the boys is pure joy. I just love their company. I am a child at heart therefore I feel at home with them. Sadly, not all family life has been so good. I have grown very distant from my two sisters.

God's Peace for all – in Christ

CHAPTER **10**

I said at the start of the book that my two aims were to think about God's peace and to cherish this peace. Whether the reader is a family member, friend or a stranger, I would like to leave you with this message.

At the time of Christ, people were obsessed with having their sins forgiven. This was a way of getting right with God. I still believe this is important today and an important part of being a Christian. We do have to be in a good and right relationship with God; we do have to live good lives and not be hypocrites. However, I like to major on what God can give us!

Jesus said many times that He wanted to give us a fantastic life. For instance, John 10:10, "....I have come that they may have life, and have it to the full. ." It really puzzles me that people don't just take God at His word. We don't have to wait till we have cancer or something similar – God has a fantastic life for us at this very moment. Many times Jesus said that we should ask for anything and it will be given. He told us to seek and even the Kingdom of God will be given to us! In Matthews Gospel, Chapter 7:7 – 8-, Jesus says, "Ask and it will be given to you, seek and you will find, knock and the door will be opened to you. For everyone who asks receives, he who seeks finds and to him who knocks the door will be opened." What great words from Jesus.

As I have said earlier, I knocked and I found. I have found Jesus to be true to His word always. Jesus has so much love for us it is incredible. Obviously, faith is the key. Why do some believe and others don't? Jesus told us to believe Him.

When we believe Jesus, His spirit personally enters into our lives. He brings forth such incredible peace and a belief that all will be well.

God is so wonderful to us. He wants us to live in His peace and have such fantastic and blessed lives. Whatever burden or problem we carry He wants to carry it, just like He carried His cross at Calvary. He wants our problems so that He can deal with them and swap them for His blessings.

I believe the whole gospel story is a complete mystery to us; the prophecies, the coming of Jesus, His death, resurrection and the coming of the Holy Spirit. However, we don't need to understand them all. There are lots of mysteries I don't understand; for example, I don't understand how a television works but I use it!

The main part of the gospel, which really means 'good news', is that we simply believe it, accept it, and try to live our lives by it. So much in life has happened by chance; inventions and so on. Christ's coming was no accident; neither was His death or resurrection. One day, as the Apostle Paul states in 1 Corinthians 13:12, "Now we see but a poor reflection as in a mirror, then we shall see face to face. Now I know in part then I shall know fully, even as I am fully known."

God knows each one of us. We are His children. He longs for us all to know Him. He wants us to walk daily with Him. Jesus has paid the penalty for the wrong things we have done; we have no need to carry guilt, and we can walk in His wonderful peace. We just have to acknowledge that Jesus is Lord and Saviour of our lives.

As with any journey, the journey starts with one step. I hope and pray this book helps the reader make or continue that step of faith.

To Follow: **Faith In Action**